The
Nixons

by
Cass R. Sandak

CRESTWOOD HOUSE
New York

Maxwell Macmillan Canada
Toronto

Maxwell Macmillan International
New York Oxford Singapore Sydney

Library of Congress Cataloging-in-Publication Data
Sandak, Cass R.
   The Nixons / by Cass R. Sandak. — 1st ed.
      p. cm. — (First families)
   Includes bibliographical references and index.
   Summary: Examines Richard and Pat Nixon as a couple, with an emphasis on their years in the White House.
   ISBN 0-89686-638-6
   1. Nixon, Richard M. (Richard Milhous), 1913–   —Juvenile literature. 2. Nixon, Pat, 1912–   —Juvenile
literature. 3. Presidents—United States—Wives—Biography—Juvenile literature. 4. Presidents—United
States—Biography—Juvenile literature. [1. Nixon, Richard M. (Richard Milhous), 1913–   . 2. Nixon, Pat,
1912–   . 3. Presidents. 4. First ladies.] I. Title. II. Series: Sandak, Cass R.   First families.
E856.S26   1992
973.924'0922—dc20
[B]   91-40216

Photo Credits
Photos courtesy of AP—Wide World Photos.

Macmillan Publishing Company	Maxwell Macmillan Canada, Inc.
866 Third Avenue	1200 Eglinton Avenue East
New York, NY 10022	Suite 200
	Don Mills, Ontario M3C 3N1

CRESTWOOD HOUSE

Macmillan Publishing Company is part of the Maxwell Communication Group of Companies.

Produced by Flying Fish Studio

Printed in the United States of America

First edition

10 9 8 7 6 5 4 3 2 1

Contents

Richard Nixon gives his farewell address as he resigns from office of president of the United States. Daughter Tricia stands behind him.

The Resignation

On August 8, 1974, President Richard M. Nixon hurriedly arranged to make a televised address to the nation. No one knew for sure what was coming. Some people, of course, thought he might resign. For two years, the hottest news item had been the Watergate scandal. Everyone wondered just how deep the president's involvement was.

But Nixon was a man always full of surprises. Some veteran reporters feared the worst: The Nixon administration might be planning a military coup. Perhaps the president was even about to declare martial law.

Just minutes into his address, Nixon made the shocking announcement:

"I shall resign the presidency at noon tomorrow."

Richard Milhous Nixon was the 37th president of the United States. He is also the only president—to date—to have resigned voluntarily. It was a sad ending to the political life of a president who had had widespread public support and overwhelming victories at the polls. But Nixon also had known defeats, both political and personal ones. He was a president who had experienced ups and downs throughout his career. Other presidents had been touched by scandal. But Richard Nixon had always proved himself to be a tough survivor through crisis after crisis.

This time, however, Nixon felt that he had let his supporters down. Although Nixon claimed he himself had done no wrong, he did admit to errors of judgment. Nixon knew that he had to resign or else face serious censure. There was no other choice.

Humble Beginnings

The president's parents, Francis and Hannah Nixon, began their married life as hardworking farmers. In 1912, with money "loaned" to him by his father-in-law, Frank Nixon had bought a lemon grove in Yorba Linda, California. It was not the last time that Hannah's parents would help the struggling couple. The lemon ranch was only ten acres, and it never produced much income. To help make ends meet, the Nixons later set up a gas station and convenience grocery store at a quiet intersection in Yorba Linda. The Nixons lived behind the store. Like the lemon grove, this enterprise was never very profitable.

Hannah Milhous had been born in Indiana in 1885. Her mother was a schoolteacher. And her father was the prosperous owner of a fruit-tree nursery. Both of Hannah's parents had attended Quaker colleges. In 1897 the Milhous family moved to the Quaker settlement of Whittier, California. It was just 46 miles east of Los Angeles.

Hannah Milhous and Francis Anthony Nixon were married on June 25, 1908. They had only known each other for four months. He was 30, she was 23. The Milhous family thought Frank Nixon was shiftless. He had left school when

Young Richard Nixon (right) *poses for this 1917 portrait.*

he was 14 and had no settled occupation. Frank had once worked as a streetcar driver, but a serious accident had cut short that career.

Frank Nixon was a Methodist, with a boisterous personality. Somehow he did not quite fit into the reserved Quaker community that Hannah's family had always known. Relatives cautioned that she was marrying beneath herself. They may have been right. People in the community remembered Frank as short-tempered and abusive to his family.

But Hannah was in love. Soon after their marriage, Frank Nixon converted to the Quaker faith. He then began to teach Sunday school. And Hannah's father tried to set his son-in-law up in the fruit-growing business.

Richard Milhous Nixon was born on January 9, 1913. To date, Nixon is the only president who was born in California. It was a freezing cold night in the neat white bungalow that Frank had built with his own hands. Richard was the Nixons' second-born son. He was to have four brothers. Two of them died in childhood, but the other two grew up to become adults. Richard's older brother, Donald, had a successful business career. His younger brother, Edward, was a naval aviation specialist and became a businessman in Seattle.

For more than three decades, Frank and Hannah Nixon continued to eke out a living. They had raised a family but had lost two of their beloved sons to disease. In 1947 Frank Nixon gave up working. It was the same time that Richard was serving his freshman year in Congress. Frank Nixon died on September 4, 1956. Nixon's mother, Hannah, died at age 82 on September 30, 1967, in a Whittier, California, nursing home.

Out of the Mouths of Babes . . .

Nixon was just a young boy in 1923 when the Teapot Dome oil reserve scandal rocked President Warren Harding's administration. People across the nation talked about the scandal. Hannah Nixon later remarked that because of the scandal her ten-year-old son, Richard, decided at this early age to become a lawyer. He promised to be "an honest one who can't be bought by crooks."

As a youngster, Richard preferred music to sports. He learned to play the piano and studied the violin. The family was poor and they lived frugally. Many nights dinner consisted of cornmeal mush.

Richard was ready to enter college in 1930. He received a scholarship from Harvard University, but the money wasn't enough to cover all the expenses. The Nixon family was still poor, and the country was just beginning to feel the pinch of the Great Depression. So Nixon settled instead for an education at nearby Whittier College. There he became an honors student and took part in many activities. Nixon was one of the leading participants in the college debating team and won fame through his skill with words. He played football with more enthusiasm than talent. He was too small to be a powerful player.

Richard Nixon (center) *as a member of the Whittier College football team*

9

Nixon graduated from Whittier in 1934 and immediately set off for law school. He had dreamed of a law career since childhood. He had been sure ever since his senior year in high school that he would become a lawyer. He won another scholarship, and this time he enrolled at Duke University Law School in North Carolina.

Nixon was as successful in law school as he had been at college. He graduated third in his class and immediately returned to California to work for a law firm in his hometown. To make his social life a little more interesting, he joined a local amateur theater group. There he met a pretty young woman called Pat Ryan.

Pat Nixon (center) *with friends on a California beach*

Thelma Ryan

If Richard Nixon's background was modest, Pat Nixon's was downright poor. She was born Catherine Thelma Patricia Ryan in Ely, Nevada, on March 16, 1912. She acquired the name Pat on the first day of her life. Her father returned from work and declared her his St. Patrick's Day baby. From then on she celebrated her birthday on March 17. She was always known as Pat.

Pat's father was an Irishman who worked in Nevada's silver mines. When Pat was two, the Ryan family picked up and moved to California. There young Pat and her brothers helped support the family by truck farming from their 11-acre plot.

Pat's German-born mother died when the young girl was only 14. Suddenly, Pat became mother, cook and cleaner for the whole family. She spent much of her time caring for her father and two older brothers. When Pat was 18, her father died of lung disease. For months she had nursed him through his final illness.

All of this hardship only made Pat a stronger person. She was determined to be hardworking and cheerful. She didn't let anything stop her from getting a first-rate education. Pat worked her way through the University of Southern California by doing odd jobs. Some of these included bit parts in Hollywood films of the 1930s. She was also an X-ray technician and schoolteacher. Pat Ryan was tall, lean and graceful. She had striking dark eyes and brown hair with a reddish tinge. By working as a salesclerk in a smart department store, she learned a lot about fashion and style. In 1937

Pat graduated from USC with honors. In that same year, Richard Nixon completed his law studies at Duke University.

The Young Couple

Pat's interest in drama got her involved with a local theater group. While the group was getting ready to perform a play called *The Dark Tower*, Pat Ryan and Richard Nixon met.

At once Richard predicted that he and Pat would eventually get married. But it wasn't until June 21, 1940, that the big event occurred. The Nixons were married at the Mission Inn in Riverside, California. Although Nixon had expected to remain a lawyer in California, he was soon offered a government job in Washington, D.C. The young couple packed up their belongings and moved East.

No sooner had they arrived in Washington than the United States entered World War II. Nixon did not believe in war or in fighting. As a Quaker, he could have been excused from serving. But he chose to ignore these beliefs and joined the navy. He was commissioned as a lieutenant. Almost immediately he went overseas. Nixon saw action in the Pacific, particularly in the Solomon Islands. During the war, Pat worked in San Francisco as an economist for the government.

By the time the war ended in 1945, Nixon had come back to the United States. It was time to decide what to do with his future. Almost by accident, a friend suggested in 1946 that Nixon run for public office. California had an open seat in the House of Representatives. It would be an uphill struggle for someone with Nixon's humble origins to embark on a career in politics. It would be difficult without the backing of a wealthy family and powerful friends.

Political Life Beckons

In order to get into the House of Representatives, Nixon had to win the seat away from Jerry Voorhis. It would be the first of many such struggles for Nixon. Voorhis was a Democrat who had once been a socialist. Nixon capitalized on this piece of information. He began a brutal campaign. During this time, the Nixons' first child, a daughter named Tricia, was born on February 21, 1946. And on Election Day in 1946, Nixon defeated Voorhis and won the first of many elections.

The election marked the beginning of pro-Nixon and anti-Nixon feelings. The split would follow Nixon throughout his political life. This first election also identified Nixon as staunchly anti-communist. The position would serve Nixon well on his first congressional committee.

One of Nixon's earliest assignments was as a member of the House Committee on Un-American Activities (HUAC). Congress had set up the committee in the aftermath of World War II. At the time, the threat of armed conflict with the Soviet Union was very real to most Americans. The Soviets had carved out a sphere of influence in Eastern Europe. And Soviet leaders seemed intent on world

13

domination through the spread of communism, the Soviet system of government. It was the beginning of a period known as the cold war.

In 1948 Nixon was sent to Europe as part of a fact-finding committee. This group needed to decide how much American money should be given to aid war-torn Europe. When Nixon returned from Europe, it was to continue his work on the HUAC. The committee's work was considered a matter of great importance for the nation's security. On July 5, 1948, in the midst of Nixon's work in Congress, Pat and Dick's second and last child, Julie, was born.

Hiss and Mudslinging

A man named Whittaker Chambers was an editor for *Time* magazine and an admitted Communist. Chambers testified before the committee that a government official named Alger Hiss was a Communist agent. Hiss had previously worked for the State Department. Hiss vehemently denied all the charges brought against him. But there was something about Hiss that bothered Nixon. Nixon hounded him until Hiss changed his story on many counts. A jury eventually convicted Hiss of lying under oath and sent him to prison for five years. Nixon's role in the affair only added to the controversy. It also established Nixon as a major political force.

In 1950 Nixon decided to run for a seat as senator from California. This time his Democratic opponent was a woman named Helen Gahagan Douglas. Married to popular actor Melvyn Douglas, she was a former singer and actress herself.

Douglas put up a good fight. But Nixon took advantage of the fact that Mrs. Douglas was both a woman and a liberal. He even suggested that she had communist leanings. There was a great deal of name-calling and mudslinging, and eventually Nixon gained his seat. Throughout the campaign, Pat Nixon was almost always at her husband's side.

Oddly, both Richard Nixon and John F. Kennedy had arrived in Washington at about the same time in 1947. Over the years, their relations were cordial. Jack Kennedy's father, Joseph Kennedy, disliked Helen Gahagan Douglas a great deal. He contributed $1,000 to Nixon's campaign to defeat her, even though the Kennedys, like the Douglases, were Democrats.

Becoming Vice President

Nixon's first big break came in 1952. Former general Dwight D. Eisenhower chose Nixon to be his vice presidential running mate in the upcoming elections. For the first time, the Nixons entered the political spotlight. In the short period of only five years, Richard Nixon had risen from the House of Representatives to vice presidential candidate. His name would soon be a household word.

Almost at once, Nixon's name and credibility were challenged—and not for the last time. He was accused of using campaign funds for his personal gain. Eisenhower and Republican party officials were unhappy about the charge. Nixon felt the need to make a public justification of

Senator Richard Nixon waves from his car during his campaign to become vice president. His wife Pat is beside him.

his expenses. He would speak to the country, and then people could decided whether or not to support him.

Nixon's speech was televised nationally. Over 58 million Americans tuned in to watch the event. Nixon gave an itemized account of his personal expenditures. He even included Pat Nixon's plain "Republican" cloth coat. During the speech, Nixon tearfully claimed that the only gift he or his family had accepted was his daughter's puppy, Checkers. Forever after, the speech would be known as Nixon's Checkers speech.

Many listeners were offended by Nixon's air of false humility. One of those people was Nixon's own mother. But others were not bothered, and the speech did nothing to tarnish Nixon's image. The general response was that Nixon had cleared his name and should be kept a part of the Republican party ticket. Eisenhower was more convinced than ever that Nixon was the right person to be his vice president.

There are some indications that it was from this point Pat Nixon developed her genuine dislike of politics. Although she always stood beside her husband, campaigned with him, appeared with him and worked on his behalf, she was not a happy political wife.

Richard and Pat Nixon with their daughters, Julie and Tricia, and family dog, Checkers

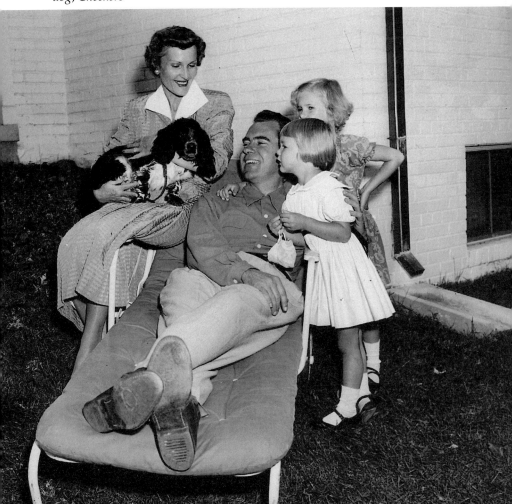

A New Vice President

Eisenhower and Nixon were successful in 1952. Their ticket won the election by a substantial 6 1/2 million vote margin. And in 1956, the pair captured another victory. Nixon was still a relatively young man of 40 when he first assumed the nation's second highest office.

The atmosphere of the Cold War was intense during the early 1950s. Rumors constantly circulated that members of the Communist party were trying to infiltrate the U.S. government. Party members had vowed to create "cells" to spread communist ideas and teaching through communist sympathizers. Hardly anyone was above suspicion.

University professors, journalists and entertainers were all subjected to humiliating questions by HUAC committee members under Wisconsin Senator Joseph McCarthy. Very much in evidence during many of these hearings was Vice President Nixon. Eisenhower had asked him to watch the proceedings closely and to keep McCarthy—who tended to be fanatical—on track. After they testified at hearings before the committee, many people were blacklisted in their professions. Often the careers and reputations of innocent people were needlessly ruined.

During his stint as vice president, Nixon became an expert at foreign policy. He observed or took part in sensitive and difficult negotiations with governments around the world. Pat accompanied him on most of these trips. During Nixon's term as vice president, he and Pat were often away from their two young daughters. Because they were devoted parents, the Nixons were always glad to get home. Despite their hectic schedules, they strongly believed in traditional family values. The Nixons tried never to let the demands of public life interfere with spending time with their children.

In September of 1955, President Eisenhower suffered a serious heart attack. For almost two months, he was unable to carry out his presidential duties. During this time, Nixon filled in for him. He never usurped the role of president but behaved with tact and dignity. In 1957 Eisenhower was again taken ill, and Nixon stood in once more. It was invaluable training for a future U.S. president.

In 1958 the Nixons made a goodwill visit to South America. It should have been a quiet, uneventful trip. But first in Peru and then later in Caracas, Venezuela, huge— and potentially dangerous—demonstrations took place. In Venezuela, particularly, the Nixons risked losing their lives when an angry crowd stormed their motorcade.

Vice President Richard Nixon looks at an anti-American sign and talks with demonstrators during his 1953 world tour.

In 1959 Nixon was sent to the Soviet Union. There he met with Soviet Premier Nikita Khrushchev in an informal "kitchen" debate. The meeting seemed to help thaw the countries' differences caused by the Cold War.

Nixon seized the vice president's role in a way that many earlier politicians had not. He turned the office into an active and dynamic position. And Americans watched him strengthen his standing within the Republican party. There was little question that Nixon would be the party's choice to succeed Eisenhower.

The First Disappointment

Nixon's years in the Eisenhower administration served him well. He had performed many key roles for the aging former general. At the Republican convention in 1960, Nixon was nominated by unanimous acclaim as the presidential candidate. Henry Cabot Lodge, a former senator from Massachusetts, was his running mate. Now a diplomat, Lodge was from an old New England family. The pair would run against the young and appealing Democrat John F. Kennedy and his running mate, Lyndon B. Johnson.

President Eisenhower (center) *with Henry Cabot Lodge* (left) *and Vice President Richard Nixon* (right)

Televised presidential debate between Senator John F. Kennedy and Vice President Richard Nixon

For the first time in an American election, television played a key role. A series of four debates between the two candidates was planned. The most important debate was the first one, and Nixon appeared tired and uncomfortable. People were riveted to their TV screens. They found John Kennedy hard to resist, while those who were only listening felt Nixon came off better. Television revealed Kennedy as a relaxed and handsome speaker, while Nixon's rough appearance and nervousness only hurt his image.

During the campaign, much was made of Kennedy's youth and vigor. But Richard Nixon was hardly an old man, being Kennedy's senior by only four years. Nixon's campaign style was very different than Kennedy's. Kennedy knew he had many obstacles to overcome, including the fact that he was a Roman Catholic. Nixon was a tireless campaigner. He traveled more than 65,000 miles and made some 180 speeches. At most of these, Pat was at his side.

Nixon and Lodge lost by a narrow margin to John F. Kennedy and Johnson. Only 120,000 votes kept Nixon from the White House. The numbers were so close that Nixon could have asked for a recount. But he didn't want to appear a sore loser. He also didn't want to cause problems for the new administration. So he accepted his defeat graciously.

For many years, Nixon would be haunted by his lack of television success. He was convinced his performance in the first TV debate had cost him the election.

The Waiting Years

In defeat Nixon took his family back to California. He returned to his law practice, but he was not happy. Nixon simply could not stay out of politics very long. In 1962 he decided to run for governor of California. He ran against the popular Democrat Edmund "Pat" Brown. Like earlier Nixon battles, the campaign was ugly. Although Nixon wanted to be back in the political spotlight, he didn't really seem to work hard enough to get there. Californians decided to go with the person they knew: Pat Brown.

Nixon's defeat was not a large one, but he took it poorly. It was after this election that Nixon told journalists at a press conference ". . .you won't have Richard Nixon to kick around anymore." If one could believe Nixon, his political career was finished. And indeed, by 1962 it seemed to many that it was.

In the months following the California defeat, Nixon wrote his first book, *Six Crises*. He itemized and then analyzed six major events in his political life and the lessons he had learned from them. They included 1) the Alger Hiss case, 2) the Checkers speech, 3) the episode in Venezuela, 4) the Eisenhower illnesses, 5) the Khrushchev meeting, and 6) the 1960 presidential campaign. Nixon reflected—and waited.

The momentum of Lyndon Johnson's Great Society campaign platform made the 1964 presidential election a disaster for the Republican party. Nixon had been by-passed to run as the presidential candidate. The party's nominee for president, Barry Goldwater, was too much of a conservative and far too right wing to appeal to many voters.

But in 1968, Nixon rose again from the ashes. The early months of the year were shattered by assassinations. First Martin Luther King, Jr., was shot down in Memphis, Tennessee. And then, just a few months later, Democratic hopeful Robert Kennedy was killed in a Los Angeles hotel.

The spring of 1968 also marked the beginning of student protests. For the first time, young Americans across the nation were outspoken and militant about what was going on. They were protesting the continuation of the Vietnam War; they were protesting civil rights violations and school policies; they were protesting just about anything.

The 1968 Republican Convention in Miami was a smooth and well-run affair. Nixon easily secured the presidential nomination. A few months later, however, the Democratic Convention in Chicago turned into a scene of mass demonstrations and riots that left many people seriously injured. There were early signs of weakness within the Democratic party—and of widespread discontent in the country.

Like the Republican Convention, Nixon's campaign was smoothly and efficiently run. By now Nixon had a group of people working on his behalf who oiled the machinery well. This time Nixon refused to debate on television, but he used television to promote his new image: honest, relaxed, likable. He defeated the Democratic candidate, Hubert Humphrey, who had served as Johnson's vice president. As in so many Nixon contests, the margin of victory was a small one. But this time it didn't really matter, because Nixon was on the winning side.

Richard Nixon and his running mate, Spiro Agnew, during the 1968 Republican Convention

The inauguration of Nixon as the president of the United States

The Oval Office
at Last

The troubled days and weeks that marked 1968 were to haunt Nixon throughout the years of his presidency. The nation grew more divided over American involvement in the Vietnam conflict. Cities were ravaged by rioting over civil rights issues and student unrest.

The twin triumphs of Nixon's presidency were ending the Vietnam War and renewing relations with the People's Republic of China. After long negotiations, the Nixon government finally ended the Vietnam War. This halfhearted war effort had sapped American resources and spirits for more than a decade. Thousands of young American men had been killed or injured. The military insisted its hands had been tied by excessive regulations and executive orders that prevented an effective war effort.

Henry Kissinger meets with Richard Nixon.

In the spring of 1970, protests against the unpopular Vietnam War reached a fever pitch on campuses across the country. At Kent State University in Ohio, four students were shot and killed and eleven were seriously injured when National Guardsmen were called in to calm the protest. Somehow the president was held personally responsible for the loss of these four young lives. Soon the same government that had entangled the country in the war was calling for an end to it.

In the same month as the Kent State tragedy, both the president's daughter Julie and her husband, David Eisenhower, graduated from college. However, because of the fear of massive protests, Julie received her degree from Smith and David his from Amherst at private family ceremonies.

Even more important was Nixon's opportunity to change Communist China's relationship with the West. In a well-publicized visit in 1972, the Nixons laid the groundwork for the People's Republic of China to enter the United Nations. The Chinese liked both Nixons and presented them with a pair of giant pandas, which were sent to the National Zoo in Washington, D.C. Many people feel that the reinstatement of U.S.-China relations was Nixon's most important achievement as president.

One of Nixon's chief advisers was Henry Kissinger. The secretary of state became a key negotiator with governments around the world, but especially in China. Secretary of State Kissinger reasoned that the most powerful nation on earth could no longer afford to ignore the world's most populous one.

Nixon was also the first to notice George Bush's potential. Nixon was instrumental in securing some important stepping-stone appointments for Bush. In 1970 Nixon appointed Bush U.S. ambassador to the United Nations. After the 1972 election, Nixon again named Bush to an important post—as head of the Republican National Committee.

The first landing on the moon took place in 1969, during Nixon's first year as president. Nixon spoke to Neil Armstrong, the first man on the moon, via radio from the Oval Office. But the groundwork for the U.S. achievement in space had been laid more than a decade before. It was, indeed, John F. Kennedy who had announced in the early 1960s that the United States would land the first astronauts on the moon before the decade was out.

Other Nixon achievements included large increases in funding to the National Endowment for the Arts. He also founded the Environmental Protection Agency (EPA) and pressed for such progressive legislation as the Clean Air Act of 1970 and the Water Quality Improvement Act.

The Nixons as First Family

The Nixons had their own style—simple, direct and fundamentally American. They were not flashy or flamboyant. Sometimes they were a little self-conscious or uncertain. Their manner was strictly Middle American. They looked like the family down the block. To many Americans, they seemed upright, religious and hardworking.

The president himself had a gruff manner and a five-o'clock shadow that seemed heavy even in the morning hours. He lacked the charisma of Kennedy or the studied smoothness of Johnson. But he spoke with passion and intensity. His political life was never squeaky clean. Several biographers have noted the disparities in Nixon's personality. They have even spoken of the "divided" man.

Nixon was a complex person. Early on he earned the nickname Tricky Dick. Many people did not trust him. But more people liked him—even if they could not explain the hold that his personality had on them.

Like her husband, Pat Nixon was very wary of the press and was never comfortable around most journalists. Mrs. Nixon was skilled at dodging questions that she did not want to answer. She could gracefully change the subject and steer the conversation to something neutral or pleasant. Nixon ordered his staff never to speak with reporters from the *New York Times* or the *Washington Post*.

The first lady went through a succession of press secretaries. This was not because Mrs. Nixon was difficult to work for, but because her husband's chief of staff, H. R. Haldeman, kept finding fault with them and their coverage of the first lady. In fact, Pat Nixon and Haldeman locked horns frequently over issues. The first lady was often angry at Haldeman's attempts to run her life as well as her family's.

The First Lady

Pat Nixon was one of Nixon's biggest political assets. She had a natural grace. She could relate easily to all races and classes of people. Mrs. Nixon was a keen analyst of the political climate and could help her husband gauge public opinion. She could be direct, but she was also sensitive and tactful. People admired Mrs. Nixon's calm and dedication, even in the face of upsetting demonstrations and attacks on her husband.

Pat Nixon relished the role of first lady, not because of the prestige but because of the chance it gave her to meet and touch the lives of so many different people. Many journalists felt that she genuinely loved and cared about people. With intelligence, style and good taste, Pat Nixon made her own mark in Washington.

Pat kept herself in good shape with a wide range of physical exercise—running, hiking, swimming and bowling. She even tried her hand at archery and throwing the javelin. With high cheekbones and well-defined features, Pat Nixon was a striking woman with a model's poise, good looks and bearing.

Pat was a serious woman who kept up with the political issues of her husband's administration by reviewing studies and briefing papers that staff members prepared for him. She wanted to be informed on policy issues.

Pat Nixon realized that with budgets for social programs stretched to their limits, only the generosity of unpaid volunteers working on all kinds of projects could really make a difference. So she became involved with the National Center for Voluntary Action and urged Congress to enact the Domestic Services Volunteer Act. She spurred efforts to organize community holiday dinners for forgotten senior citizens who had no families.

A Life on the Go

While Richard Nixon was president, Pat Nixon visited many parts of the country and the world. During her husband's first term alone, she visited 39 of the 50 states. Pat Nixon was the most traveled first lady until Barbara Bush came along. Her role was similar to that of Franklin Roosevelt's first lady, Eleanor Roosevelt. Pat Nixon was able to observe and relate to people in a way that her husband could not. Even so, Mrs. Nixon admitted that she would not have chosen a life in politics.

Early in Nixon's first term, Pat's initial trip as first lady took her on a tour of many Asian nations. The trip also included a brief, unannounced visit with her husband to the Vietnam War zone. While President Nixon met with the president of war-torn South Vietnam, Pat Nixon toured the battle zone in an open helicopter, viewing U.S. troops positioned in the jungle below. She was on her way to visit wounded soldiers in a U.S. military hospital.

Important state visits took the Nixons to the Soviet Union and China as U.S. relations with those countries improved. In her role as the president's personal envoy, the first lady made visits to Africa and South America, unaccompanied by her husband.

President Nixon shakes hands with Communist Party Chief Leonid Brezhnev after the two leaders signed a treaty to work toward total world disarmament.

Over Memorial Day weekend in 1970, there was a massive earthquake in Peru. It left 80,000 people dead and close to a million homeless. One week later, Mrs. Nixon was on a plane headed for Lima. She brought with her tons of donated food, clothing and medical supplies. She became the darling of the South American press. Her effort was not only a tremendous humanitarian gesture but also a wise political move.

On official foreign tours, Pat Nixon usually insisted on following her own agenda, scheduling visits to hospitals, schools and social service organizations. There she could meet with people—both those in need and those who could make things happen. As a young schoolteacher, Pat Nixon had worked with poor and underprivileged Mexican-American children. Her warmth and directness were appreciated.

The Family Circle

Pat Nixon remained a mystery to almost everyone because she almost never shared her private feelings. She was a quiet and reflective woman who genuinely disliked the limelight. She was not shy, but she loved her solitude. She had no close friends beyond Helene Drown, a lifelong friend from California with whom she kept in touch. Her daughters and her husband were the only other people in whom she confided.

The Nixons enjoyed a close family life with their daughters. Several evenings a week were reserved for special candlelit dinners with the family. Often there was music.

Mrs. Nixon had been the family disciplinarian, but her daughters remained close to her. They interacted more as friends than as parents and children. At White House functions, Tricia and Julie often pitched in to help the first lady. They shared in plans and mingled with guests at White House social events.

Even before her father was sworn in as president, Julie Nixon announced her engagement to David Eisenhower, former President Eisenhower's grandson. With their subsequent marriage in New York City, two of America's most powerful political families were united.

The Nixons had been close to the Eisenhower family ever since Nixon's eight years as vice president. When former President Eisenhower suffered his final illness, the Nixons became like a second family to Mrs. Eisenhower. From then on, Mamie usually spent Christmases at the White House with the Nixons.

Tricia Nixon was married to Edward Cox in June 1971. The service took place in the Rose Garden of the White House. It was also the first wedding to take place on the grounds of the White House.

Tricia's White House wedding made headlines. The country was sick of hearing about Vietnam, and the public was glad to see a pretty girl marry a dashing marine in a fairy-tale wedding. Included on the guest list was Theodore Roosevelt's daughter, Alice Roosevelt Longworth, who had been married in a 1905 ceremony at the White House.

The Nixon White House

Mrs. Nixon wanted the nation to feel that the White House belonged to them. She promoted a more relaxed kind of tourism at the historic mansion. She frequently came downstairs from the private family quarters to greet visitors and to chat, shake hands and pose for photographs.

When a group of poor Appalachian women came to the White House to meet with the first lady, they were so overcome with anxiety that they burst into tears. Pat Nixon put the women at ease when she gently threaded her way through the group. She stopped to hug each one and offered words of encouragement.

Pat Nixon established candlelight tours of the White House during the Christmas season. Pat felt that this was necessary because so many people could not visit the White House during the daytime. She also favored more homey Christmas decorations and often supervised them personally. In 1969 the Nixons sent some 37,000 Christmas cards to friends and dignitaries.

At Christmas Pat pitched in to help electricians and workmen decorate the White House. She climbed up ladders and hammered away. Afterward she warmly invited the workers to join her for cookies and eggnog. Mrs. Nixon always made sure that the family Christmas dinner was served early enough in the day so that staff members could get home to their families.

Pat Nixon started garden tours of the White House grounds. She also supervised preparation of new pamphlets and guidebooks to describe the house and its history. She worked with engineers to come up with an exterior lighting scheme that would show off the house and its architectural features. She created a map room, did extensive renovation to the China room and worked on restoring other rooms in the mansion. Through Mrs. Nixon's efforts, almost 300 fine antiques were added to the White House collection.

One of Pat Nixon's special causes was White House restoration. Here she was following in the tradition established by Jacqueline Kennedy and other first ladies. But Pat Nixon has received little credit for all the painstaking work she did.

In her five years at the White House, Pat Nixon supervised a great deal of decoration work on the public rooms on the ground floor and the first floor. She also worked hard to fill in gaps in the collection of presidential and first-lady portraits. She was able to obtain priceless portraits of Louisa Adams and Dolley Madison. And she hosted the simple private ceremony when Jacqueline Onassis and her children returned to the White House for the official presentation of the portraits of John F. Kennedy and Mrs. Kennedy.

The First Couple

Many observers have thought that the Nixon marriage was a cold one. In public the two seemed reserved. They were rarely seen even chatting to one another. Once a photographer caught the first couple strolling arm in arm down the same California beach where Richard Nixon had first proposed marriage.

But Mrs. Nixon described her husband as sentimental. He showered her with praise and frequent gifts. One of the few personal items Nixon kept in his office at the White House was a ceramic elephant that Pat had given him during their courtship. Birthdays, anniversaries and other special days were always remembered.

People close to the couple felt that the president idolized and adored his wife. He acknowledged his debt to her and realized how important the first lady could be in reaching people the president might overlook. Nixon also wanted to spare her the difficulties of life in the public eye. Mrs. Nixon hated it when people criticized her husband. She was sensitive to his vulnerability and his childhood memories.

The president hated others being late. But Pat was strong willed enough to keep the president waiting when she needed extra time. Pat was a fanatic about cleanliness and even banished the family dogs from the Nixons' living quarters. Mrs. Nixon was a good sport who did not expect to be waited on hand and foot. She packed her own suitcases for her frequent trips and insisted on keeping her own schedule.

The Nixons had separate bedrooms in the White House. Pat Nixon kept regular hours but needed her rest. Her husband suffered from insomnia and would often get up during the night to jot down notes or speak into a tape recorder.

The first lady spent about four hours each day working on correspondence. She received more than 300 letters each week. Most of them were favorable words from admirers.

She also received and responded to many desperate pleas for help from people who needed counseling and from those who needed assistance in finding jobs or in dealing with government red tape.

Pat usually worked at a desk in her dressing room. She answered mail and phone messages promptly. Her staff always found her accessible. The first lady did not keep a journal, but she did keep a record of conversations and events by making shorthand notes on her engagement calendar.

President Nixon may have sprung from humble beginnings, but he easily learned to savor the fruits of success. As chief executive, he had nine personal offices. They were spread across the country. He had luxurious family retreats in both Florida and California. He also oversaw more than $17 million worth of improvements made to these properties.

At White House dinners, the staff served guests with wine that cost $6 a bottle, while the president's own glass was always filled from an unmarked carafe of vintage wine costing $30 a bottle. It was a comfortable lifestyle, and the family enjoyed it hugely. But then something happened.

The Beginning of the End

It all began simply enough. Nixon was frightened that he wasn't going to win the 1972 election. He was running against Democrat George McGovern, a senator from South Dakota. McGovern was not a particularly inspiring candidate, but he had broad liberal appeal. Nixon even set up a special organization, the Committee for the Reelection of the President (known as CREEP). Many of the organization's strategies depended on wire tapping, bugging and the wholesale invasion of privacy.

President Nixon announces the end of the Vietnam War.

On June 19, 1972, five men were arrested as they tried to break into the Democratic National Committee headquarters at the Watergate hotel and apartment complex in Washington, D. C. The five men were Republicans. And it turned out that they were actually entering the premises for the second time. This time they were there to repair some electronic bugging equipment that had failed to work. Some of the people involved in the break-in were part of CREEP.

From the beginning, Nixon disavowed any knowledge of what had happened. No one knows if this was true or not. What is likely, though, is that if Nixon had stepped forward and disciplined these people, his presidency could have been saved. But, for whatever reasons, Nixon did nothing.

From a simple burglary grew one of the greatest scandals in the history of the United States. Not long after Nixon's second inauguration, the Watergate hearings began. As allegation followed allegation, Nixon began to retreat into his own world. The hearings lasted more than a year. Relations between the Nixons became strained, and the first family experienced a growing sense of despair.

With each new stage of the investigation, more and more facts were made public. John Ehrlichman, head of Nixon's domestic council, and H. R. Haldeman seemed to be involved in the crisis on many levels. And they were the men closest to the president. But Nixon still refused to do anything.

Tapes that had been recorded in secret in the president's Oval Office were made public. There was not much secret

Richard Nixon with Secretary of State Henry Kissinger, Vice President Gerald Ford and Alexander Haig

information on them, but the coarseness of the conversation and some offensive language helped to destroy Nixon's lofty reputation.

Television came back to haunt Nixon during the Watergate crisis. In 1973 and 1974, the televised Watergate hearings became a way of life for many Americans.

In the midst of the Watergate crisis, Vice President, Spiro Agnew was forced to resign. Charges were made that, as governor of Maryland, he had accepted large kickbacks from campaign supporters. These charges proved to be true. On October 12, 1973, Gerald Ford was chosen to replace Agnew as vice president.

Events Leading up to the Resignation

The shadow over the presidency continued to grow. By midsummer 1974, the Watergate hearings had gone so far that it seemed as if impeachment of the president was inevitable. "Impeachment" means simply that a formal accusation will be leveled at the president. In itself, impeachment is not a conviction of guilt. Still, the proceedings had gone far enough. In order for his accusers to bring a case against the president of the United States, they had to be sure their evidence was very strong.

That the highest official in the country would be accused of involvement in a serious criminal act was bad enough. To suffer through this process would bring personal humiliation to every Nixon family member. Even if Nixon were acquitted in the end, the revelations made during the trial could prove damaging.

By August 2, the president confided to his daughter Julie his decision to resign. Julie had the sad task of breaking the news to her mother. Mrs. Nixon was in her bedroom. The two women talked for a while, shed a few tears, and then Pat began packing. In just a week, the Nixons would be moving out of the White House forever.

On the night of August 7, Nixon had finished drafting his resignation speech. The family gathered for their last dinner in the White House. Pat stayed up all night packing.

Faced with the realities of the situation, on August 8, 1974, President Nixon announced to the nation by means of a televised statement his decision to resign the presidency on August 9. In his address, he expressed the hope that his action would lead to "that process of healing which is so desperately needed in America."

Following a farewell speech to his White House staff on August 9, the Nixons descended the stairs. They then met Gerald and Betty Ford, who were waiting downstairs. The two couples headed out to the White House lawn. There a helicopter was waiting to take the Nixons to an airplane. They boarded Air Force One and were winging their way to California when Nixon ceased to be president.

Nixon apparently remained firm in his belief that he had not obstructed justice in his conduct throughout the Watergate affair. His decision to resign came as a devastating blow to his family. His daughters urged him to fight it out and to submit to the impeachment process. They were confident of his innocence. But with his usual passion and intensity, Nixon chose to step down.

Nixon addresses his staff at the White House for the last time.

Life After Watergate

Pat Nixon took her husband's resignation probably the hardest of all. She felt the family's shame and could not seem to forgive herself for what had happened. The couple retired to La Casa Pacifica, their San Clemente home. There Pat led the life of a woman in exile. She became something of a recluse, almost never leaving home.

To many people's surprise—and some people's horror—President Ford pardoned Nixon almost a month after he left the White House. This meant he could not be prosecuted for any crimes he might have committed in connection with the Watergate affair.

Nixon's closest aides, however, did not escape from the Watergate scandal unscathed. Haldeman and Ehrlichman were both forced to resign. And several other top employees served brief jail sentences in minimum security prisons for their roles in the break-in.

In the months immediately following their move from the White House, Pat and Dick communicated by means of tersely written notes carried between the two by Nixon's personal secretary. And the stress and strain continued. In 1976 Pat Nixon suffered a stroke that left her partially paralyzed. Because of her illness and also because she was a reluctant first lady, Pat Nixon has kept almost completely out of the public eye.

In contrast, immediately following his resignation, Nixon set to work reconstructing his image and reputation. He wrote books and appeared on major television talk shows. For these appearances, he received large sums of

Former President and Mrs. Nixon with their daughters, Julie and Tricia, on the occasion of the Nixons' 50th wedding anniversary in 1990.

44

money. Some people felt that Nixon should not be making a profit from what were seen as his crimes.

Almost two decades after his unprecedented resignation, Nixon's reputation as a shrewd and effective public figure has been largely restored. He may be viewed as something of a tragic figure caught up by events no longer under his control—but he is no longer perceived as a dishonest politician who deliberately misled his country and betrayed the trust it placed in him.

After spending a few years in relative seclusion on the West Coast, the Nixons moved to Saddle River, New Jersey, to be closer to their daughters and grandchildren. As time passes, wounds heal. And perhaps history's judgment on the Nixons will be kinder than the harsh feelings that sent them from the White House in 1974.

For Further Reading

Anthony, Carl Sferrazza. *First Ladies: The Saga of the Presidents' Wives and Their Power, 1961–1990*. New York: William Morrow and Company, Inc., 1991.

Eisenhower, Julie Nixon. *Pat Nixon, The Untold Story*. New York: Simon & Schuster, 1986.

Friedel, Frank. *The Presidents of the United States of America*. Revised edition. Washington, D.C.: The White House Historical Association, 1989.

Klapthor, Margaret Brown. *The First Ladies*. Revised edition. Washington, D.C.: The White House Historical Association, 1989.

Larsen, Rebecca. *Richard Nixon, Rise and Fall of a President*. New York: Franklin Watts, 1991.

Lillegard, Dee. *Encyclopedia of Presidents: Richard Nixon*. Chicago: Children's Press, 1988.

Nadel, Laurie. *The Great Stream of History. A Biography of Richard Nixon*. New York: Atheneum, 1991.

St. George, Judith. *The White House: Cornerstone of a Nation*. New York: G. P. Putnam's Sons, 1990.

Stefoff, Rebecca. *Richard M. Nixon. 37th President of the United States*. Ada, Okla.: Garrett Educational Corporation, 1990.

Index